by

Charlie Ogden

Crabtree Publishing Company
www.crabtreebooks.com
1-800-387-7650

Published in Canada
Crabtree Publishing
616 Welland Avenue
St. Catharines, ON
L2M 5V6

Published in the United States
Crabtree Publishing
PMB 59051
350 Fifth Ave, 59th Floor
New York, NY 10118

Published by Crabtree Publishing Company in 2017

First Published by Book Life in 2016
Copyright © 2017 Book Life

Author
Charlie Ogden

Editors
Grace Jones
Janine Deschenes
Ellen Rodger

Design
Drue Rintoul

Proofreader
Crystal Sikkens

**Production coordinator and
prepress technician (interior)**
Margaret Amy Salter

Prepress technician (covers)
Ken Wright

Print coordinator
Katherine Berti

Printed in Hong Kong/012017/BK20161024

Photographs
Shutterstock: Olga Besnard: cover (top); paul prescott: page 6; HUANG Zheng: page 7; William Perugini: page 8; 501room: page 11; Ollyy page: 13; Andresr: page 17 (left); g-stockstudio: page 17 (right); BeeZeePhoto: page 21; Leonard Zhukovsky: page 25; J. Bicking: page 27; J. Bicking; page 28; studiolaska: page 29

All other images from Shutterstock and Wikimedia Commons.

Cover Images
(Top) PARIS - Gay Pride parade in Paris, France, in 1010, in support of equal rights for gay people.
(Bottom) American pilot Amelia Earhart challenged gender roles in the 1930s at a time when there were few female pilots and women typically wore skirts not pants and other masculine clothing.

Library and Archives Canada Cataloguing in Publication

Ogden, Charlie, author
    Identity and gender / Charlie Ogden.

(Our values)
Issued in print and electronic formats.
ISBN 978-0-7787-3268-6 (hardcover).--
ISBN 978-0-7787-3369-0 (paperback).--
ISBN 978-1-4271-1899-8 (html)

    1. Identity (Psychology)--Juvenile literature. 2. Gender identity--Juvenile literature. I. Title.

BF697.O33 2016   j155.2   C2016-906670-3
                                        C2016-906671-1

Library of Congress Cataloging-in-Publication Data

CIP available at Library of Congress

CONTENTS

Words in **bold** can be found in the glossary on page 31.

WHAT IS IDENTITY?

Every person on the planet has an identity. Identities are the views that people have of themselves. They include the way people see themselves in relation to other people. People's identities are often tied to the roles that they hold at home, at school or work, and in their community. The things a person believes in, and feels strongly about, also makes up a large part of their identity. A person's identity is not always something that you can see. In fact, in a lot of cases, a person chooses to keep certain parts of their identity to themselves. Identities grow and can change over time. They can be shaped by a lot of things—some that you can control, and some that you can't control. Your identity is the collection of things that make you, you!

Your identity is the view that you have of yourself.

IDENTITY THROUGH TIME

A person's identity often takes a long time to develop and be fully understood. This is because a person needs to know a lot about themselves before they can really understand their identity and who they are as a person. People often take time to decide or realize the things that are important to them or what they believe in. For example, a person might learn about pollution at school and decide to get involved to help the environment. They could realize that environmental **activism** is an important part of their identity. Your identity can grow and change over time. Something that was important to someone at one point in their life may not be part of their identity later. It's normal for people's beliefs and interests to change as they learn and grow.

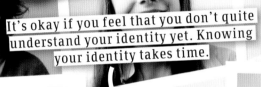

It's okay if you feel that you don't quite understand your identity yet. Knowing your identity takes time.

GROUP IDENTITIES

Sometimes a person can gain a sense of who they are through the groups they belong to. These may include family, religious, ethnic, or even sports or hobby groups. These groups help give a person a sense of belonging and a **social identity**.

These people all follow the religion of Hinduism. They make up a group identity.

One of the most common ways that people can share a group identity is through religion. People who follow the same religion have a group identity. They share beliefs about the world and how they should live their lives. However, having a group identity does not mean that you have the exact same identity as someone else. Everyone's identity is special and **unique** to them. This means that a person can have their own personal identity and share a group identity at the same time.

ANIMAL RIGHTS ACTIVISM

One example of a group that many people identify with is animal rights activism. People who care about animal rights believe that there should be laws to stop people from mistreating animals. In many places around the world, animals live in terrible conditions. They are kept in very small cages and are sometimes not given enough food or water. They often live their whole life in a cage before being killed to eat for food. Animal rights activists share very strong beliefs about animal rights. They band together and attend events such as protests. This strengthens their sense of social identity because it makes each individual feel they belong to a shared cause, or something bigger than themselves.

Animal rights activists often hold **protests** to raise awareness about the mistreatment of animals.

WHAT SHAPES YOUR IDENTITY?

A person's identity can be shaped by a range of different things. Experiences, people, places, backgrounds, and cultures can all influence someone's identity. Identities are shaped by things you can control, such as the type of music you listen to. They are also shaped by things you can't control, such as where you grew up. Identity can even be influenced by things you read about, see on television, or hear about from others.

Sometimes, people's identities are shaped by the things they learn about on the Internet, at school, or from others. Things that influence someone's identity don't always have to come from personal experience.

It can be difficult to identify all of the things that have helped shape your identity. To help understand our identities, it can be helpful to practice self reflection, which means to look back or think carefully about one's thoughts and actions. Looking back on our experiences, backgrounds, beliefs, and interests can help us understand the things that are important to us. These are some of the things that make up our identities.

PASSIONS

A person's passions are the things that they are most enthusiastic, or excited, about. Everybody has passions—whether they are sports, music, books, traveling, or animals. Often, a person's passions make up a large part of their identity. For example, people who are very passionate about music will often make music a part of their identity. They may do this by becoming musicians and practicing music in their spare time.

The things that we are interested in and passionate about can often change as we grow older. This is how your identity can develop and grow over time. As your passions change, certain parts of your identity change as well. While certain aspects of your identity will change, grow, and develop, many people believe that there is a part that will always stay the same. It is this part of your identity that makes you unique, and it is based on all of your personal experiences and beliefs.

FAMILIES

Members of your family will often have a big influence on your identity. This is because our family members teach us a lot about life and how the world works. Our families are also often the people who first expose us to beliefs and traditions.

One way that parents and guardians can shape the identities of their children is by helping them to understand what is right and wrong. By helping children develop these beliefs, they are teaching them morals and ethics.

Parents and guardians also often pass on their passions to their children. For example, if baking is part of your father's identity, it might become part of yours, too!

CULTURES

Cultures are the ideas, customs, and behaviors that a group of people share and practice. Cultures often involve the food that people eat, the festivals they celebrate, the languages they speak, and the ways they act. A person's culture will often come from the community in which they grew up.

People often acquire their cultural identity from their family. Our families are usually the first people to teach us about our ancestry and culture. They pass on cultural traditions and beliefs.

Sharing the same culture is another way people may identify with a group. People from the same culture may follow the same religion, celebrate the same festivals, and take part in the same customs. A person's culture usually involves many things that they believe are important, which is why culture often becomes a part of a person's identity. When people have a group identity through their shared culture, they have a cultural identity.

Paper lanterns are an important part of Japanese culture.

PROMOTING SELF-ACCEPTANCE

Self-acceptance is a person's happiness with who they are. It usually means that a person needs to understand themselves and accept their strengths and their weaknesses. When a person practices self-acceptance, they know that their weaknesses do not make them who they are. They accept all parts of their identity.

The first step to practicing self-acceptance is to think about what makes up your identity. It can be very difficult to understand how we feel and what our identity is. It's normal to feel this way, and we can ask for help to work through these challenges from the people we trust. A good way to start can be to think about the things you enjoy and the things that are important to you. Understanding our own identities is the beginning of self-acceptance. When we know how to accept ourselves, we can also show others acceptance.

Being happy with who you are involves being happy with the way that you act and the things that you do. A helpful way to begin practicing self-acceptance is to figure out the things that are important to you. Once you have determined your values, you can start to do things that support them. For example, Zoe feels that helping others is a very important part of who she is. She feels happy when she helps others. Zoe knows that one of her skills is in math, so she decides to start a math club at school. The people in the club give homework help to younger students. Since helping others is part of Zoe's identity, the club helps her feel proud of who she is. Another good way to promote self-acceptance is to think about the goals you have for yourself in the future. Working hard and achieving goals helps people feel happy with who they are. A big part of self-acceptance is knowing the things that you want to achieve, and working hard to achieve them despite any obstacles.

VALUES

Living your life according to the values that you believe in is one of the best ways to be happy with who you are. Values are things that people feel strongly about, just like passions. However, values are different from passions. Values are principles, or how a person acts and what they believe is right. A person's values are the types of behavior that they think are most important, such as telling the truth, being kind, and treating people with **respect**. Our values often make up part of our identities.

Many people believe that kindness and generosity are important values to live by.

It's important to figure out the values that are most important to you and to try to put them into practice in your day-to-day life. One of Michael's values is to show respect for others. He tries to be respectful to others every day. Respectful behavior includes following through on a commitment or listening to others' opinions without interrupting. Michael understands that part of his identity is being a respectful person.

14

CELEBRATING DIFFERENCES

We all have different qualities, backgrounds, and skills. There are some things that we cannot change, such as where we were born. Understanding and accepting that there are things about yourself that you can't change is a very important part of being happy with who you are. It's normal to not like something about yourself—but understanding that everyone is unique, and celebrating our differences, can help us have a positive view of our identities.

It is important for people to embrace the things about themselves that they think make them different. Everyone in the world is unique, so of course people are different from one another! What is important is to learn to celebrate the things that make us different and accept ourselves for who we are.

WHAT IS GENDER?

Gender is one of the most important and complex identities. That's because gender is so **diverse**. Gender is different from sex. When we are born, we are **assigned** a sex. This assignment, usually girl or boy, is based on a quick **biological** inspection of a newborn baby's body parts. But even this can be confusing. There are more than two options for sex. Babies can be born female, male, or intersexed, meaning they belong to both sexes. Gender refers to how a person feels about themselves, their identity, and how they express their identity. There are also different genders. People can identify, or see themselves, as one or more genders.

The ideal image of the female gender in the mid to late 1800s was known as the "Angel in the House." This term was intended to show that most women were expected to marry a man. Married women were supposed to do as they were told and be entirely devoted to their husbands.

Gender roles are behaviors and actions considered appropriate or desirable for people based on their gender. These roles are **socially constructed**, or determined by the culture and society we live in. They lay out how people of a certain gender should act. Over time, these roles have change. Many people may act in ways that are not determined by their sex or gender. In many places, people can be free to express, or show, their gender in ways that do not follow gender roles.

The terms "masculine" and "feminine" are often used to describe the male and female genders. If something is masculine, then it relates to the male gender. If something is feminine, then it relates to the female gender.

When talking about sex, the term "man" or "boy" is used to describe the male sex and the term "woman" or "girl" is used to describe the female sex. However, not every person identifies themselves with one of these words.

From the day babies are born, we socially construct their gender. Boy babies are stereotypically dressed in blue, and girls in pink.

Gender has nothing to do with our physical attributes or our sex. Instead, gender is determined by each person's relationship with the societies and cultures that are important to them. A person who is biologically male may not feel being masculine is part of their identity. They may prefer to not be called a man. It is important to understand the difference between sex and gender and respect others' gender identities.

IDENTITY AND GENDER

Identity and gender are very closely linked. A person's gender often makes up a large part of their identity. This is called someone's gender identity. A person's **gender identity** may or may not line up with their sex.

A person can identify their gender as male, female, and other variations such as genderqueer. Genderqueer is a term for gender identities outside of male and female such as bigender, in which a person's gender identity flows between male and female, and agender, in which a person does not identify with any gender.

Gender identity is a person's internal sense of themselves. The way a person looks does not always indicate their gender identity. Gender expression is how a person presents, or shows, their gender publicly. For example, if a person believes that being feminine is an important part of their identity, they might express this by wearing **conventionally** feminine clothing such as dresses. Group identities can also be built around gender identities. For example, a group of boys who play very physical sports may share a masculine gender identity, because masculinity is often associated with being physically strong. Sometimes people express themselves as gender non-binary, gender-expansive, or genderqueer. These are self-identifying terms for people who do not see themselves as just masculine or feminine. It is important to respect everyone's gender identity.

GENDER IDENTITY

A person's gender identity is the way they feel about, identify, and perceive their own gender. Just like a regular identity, a person's gender identity often involves a lot of their beliefs, values, passions, likes, and dislikes. A gender identity is a person's own experience of their gender and the way they interact with the world.

The Thai flag

Thailand has one of the most accepting societies in the world in relation to gender identities. Views about masculinity and femininity aren't very strict in the country and people are mostly free to express their gender identity however they please.

For many people, understanding their gender identity can be difficult, upsetting, and take a long time. This is because many people believe that men should be masculine and women should be feminine. If a person's gender identity does not follow those beliefs, it can be difficult for them and others to understand. However, a lot of people now recognize that gender and sex are two very different things. Wherever you live in the world, it is important that you support people who are struggling with their gender identity so that they feel safe and respected to explore and express themselves in a way they feel most comfortable.

THE GENDER SPECTRUM

For a long time, people thought that a person's gender could be only one of two things. They believed a person had to be either masculine or feminine, because a person's gender was the same as their assigned biological sex.

Today, many people accept that gender should be thought of as a **spectrum**. People do not have to identify their gender as being the same as their sex. They do not have to be completely masculine or completely feminine.

The color spectrum

To better understand what the gender spectrum means, look at the color spectrum. The left end of the spectrum is red, and the right end is violet. To say that a person's gender is only masculine or feminine is like saying that the only colors are violet and red. As we can see from this color spectrum, there are many colors in between red and violet. In the same way, people can identify their genders as falling anywhere between masculine and feminine. As a person's gender isn't related to their biological sex, it is possible for a person's gender to fall anywhere on this spectrum.

The gender spectrum allows for many different expressions of gender, because a person's gender can fall anywhere on the spectrum. Some people identify themselves as genderqueer. A person who is genderqueer or gender non-binary may identify with two or more genders. They may also be genderfluid, which means they have a gender identity that changes. Some people may consider themselves nongender, agender, or genderfree. This means they don't identify with any gender. Genderqueer people might express their gender in traditionally masculine or feminine ways, or in ways that are seen as both. There are many people who are biologically male, but consider their gender identity to be female. In the same way, many people who are biologically female consider their gender identity to be male. These people are known as transgender. The gender spectrum can help us understand how transgender people view their gender identity. It is important to respect others' gender identities and call them by the names and **pronouns**, such as him or her, that they identify with. Everyone should have the right to express their gender identity without facing **discrimination**.

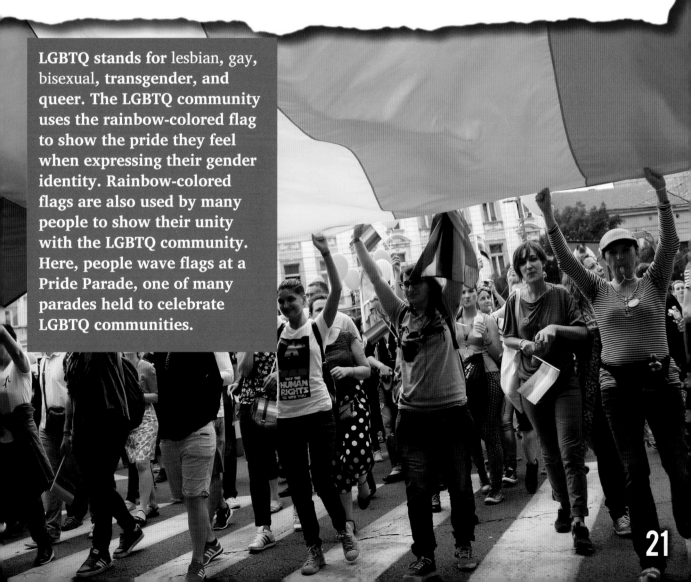

LGBTQ stands for lesbian, gay, bisexual, **transgender, and queer. The LGBTQ community uses the rainbow-colored flag to show the pride they feel when expressing their gender identity. Rainbow-colored flags are also used by many people to show their unity with the LGBTQ community. Here, people wave flags at a Pride Parade, one of many parades held to celebrate LGBTQ communities.**

HISTORY OF
GENDER IDENTITY

As our society changes, so do our ideas about gender and gender roles. In many cultures, gender has historically been viewed as either male or female. These two options were based on the sex a child was assigned at birth. The child had no say in this. If a person grew up feeling that their gender was different from their assigned sex, they usually had to hide their feelings. They pretended to be someone they weren't, as expressing their identity could be very dangerous.

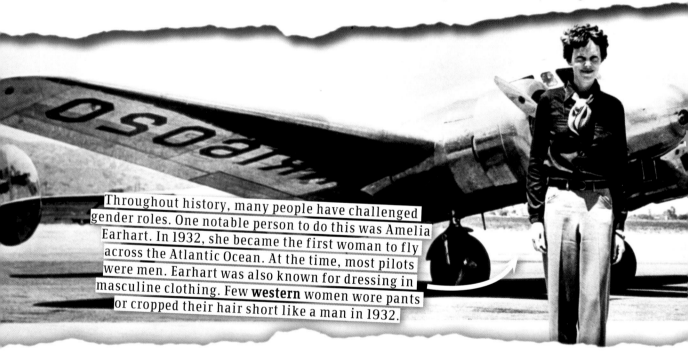

Throughout history, many people have challenged gender roles. One notable person to do this was Amelia Earhart. In 1932, she became the first woman to fly across the Atlantic Ocean. At the time, most pilots were men. Earhart was also known for dressing in masculine clothing. Few **western** women wore pants or cropped their hair short like a man in 1932.

Gender and gender roles are taught to us from the time of our births. We learn it at home, in schools, through religion, culture, and media. For some people, this works because the commonly accepted ideas of gender fit with who they are. But many people struggle to live up to gender roles. Going against gender roles has always been risky because people who accept **dominant** gender roles can feel threatened when their behaviors are challenged. For example, around 100 years ago it was believed that a woman's role was to care for her family at home. Women who protested for the right to vote in public were criticized by men and other women who were satisfied with following the gender roles at the time.

Gender roles change through time and culture. In ancient Greece and Rome, a person's gender was considered either male or female. Both were patriarchal societies where men had more power and authority over all things, including women. Most of our ideas of gender roles come from these ancient societies.

Some ancient cultures had other ideas and beliefs of gender that were closer to the gender spectrum we know today. For example, the Bugis people of Indonesia have five separate genders, including one, called bissu, that refers to people born as both male and female.

THE ANCIENT ROMAN GOD OF LOVE, CUPID, WAS OCCASIONALLY DEPICTED AS BEING INTERSEX, OR PHYSICALLY BOTH MALE AND FEMALE. THIS REVEALS THAT SOME ANCIENT SOCIETIES RECOGNIZED PEOPLE OF DIFFERENT GENDER IDENTITIES.

Many cultures accept that gender is not binary, or consisting of just male and female. Some Asian and African societies believed transgender people were priests or priestesses who possessed higher knowledge. In some **indigenous** North American communities, Two-Spirit is a term for people whose gender identity is fluid. These people were historically given special respect. Today, some countries acknowledge multiple gender identities in laws. In Australia, people can choose X as their gender or sex on birth certificates and passports. This means they are neither male or female.

When communities began moving toward patriarchal systems, in which men were in charge, people with queer gender identities were commonly discriminated against by their community. Many of the civilizations that became powerful throughout history thought that men were better than women, which led to a lot of people being discriminated against for their sex and gender. In these societies, women were always worse off than men, no matter what their gender identity was. Men who didn't conform to strict gender roles suffered as well. They were expected to behave in masculine ways. This meant dressing a certain way, and working in masculine careers. If men didn't, they were ridiculed or punished.

OSCAR WILDE, A FAMOUS VICTORIAN PLAYWRIGHT, POET, AND AUTHOR, WAS ONE OF THE FIRST PUBLIC FIGURES TO CHALLENGE SOCIAL VIEWS ABOUT GENDER IN HIS WORK AND IN REAL LIFE.

The history of transgender and gender non-conforming people has largely been hidden. Some of it has been recorded and **suppressed**, or lost. In some societies, they were afraid to express their gender identities for fear of discrimination or violence. There are some individuals, however, that challenged the idea that men had to be masculine and women had to be feminine. Over time, the number of people who identified as genderqueer grew, and they began to speak out and fight for their right to express their identities without discrimination.

LGBTQ RIGHTS MOVEMENTS

Around the time of the 1950s, 1960s, and 1970s, movements and organizations that fought for LGBTQ rights started to gain attention in the United States and Canada. The first organizations for gay and lesbian rights were created in the United States in the 1950s. These groups worked to **decriminalize** same-sex relationships in the country. Illinois became the first state to decriminalize **homosexuality** in 1962. In Canada, homosexuality was decriminalized in 1969.

In 1969, the Stonewall riots put gay rights on the map. The Stonewall Inn was a bar where gay and lesbian people often spent time together. When it was raided by the police, gay, lesbian, and trans people fought back, saying that they were being targeted for who they were. The Stonewall riots are said to represent gay pride, and are celebrated every year with the Pride parade held around the world in June.

After the Stonewall riots, movements for LGBTQ rights began to grow across North America. In the United States, openly gay politicians such as Harvey Milk and Elaine Noble were elected to office. Milk was elected to the San Francisco Board of Supervisors and Noble to the Massachussets House of Representatives. In Canada, from 1977 to 1998, provincial human rights codes were changed to include gay rights. Gay marriage became legal across Canada in 2005, and the United States in 2015.

GENDER IDENTITY TODAY

Governments from all around the world have passed gender equality laws. These laws are an attempt to give people of any gender equal rights, equal opportunities, and an equal status in their country. In the United States and Canada, it is illegal for someone to be refused a job or an education based on their gender identity. In many countries, people of any gender have the right to marry.

In recent years, many people have joined the gender neutrality movement. This is the idea that laws and language should avoid distinguishing between different genders as this promotes the belief that there are only two genders, rather than a spectrum.

The Indian flag

Governments have begun to recognize transgender rights. Some have passed new laws that acknowledge there are more than two genders. One of these countries is India, which, in 2014, made "transgender" the country's third official gender.

The Indian government did this because they believed that a person's gender identity is a core part of their right to freedom. This means that people should always feel free to express their gender, no matter where their gender falls on the spectrum.

TRANSGENDER RIGHTS

There have been many advancements in the LGBTQ community, allowing many people to express their gender identities legally. But some genderqueer people—especially transgender people—must continually fight for their rights. In recent years, people who are transgender have faced great discrimination in society. A lot of the time, people do not understand what it is like to be a transgender person, so they do not feel that they need rights to express their identities.

These people gathered in North Carolina in order to protest for the rights of transgender people. In March 2016, the state banned transgender people from using bathrooms that followed their gender identity.

In some areas of the United States, a transgender person is not recognized by their gender of choice if they have not had surgery that changes the way their body biologically looks. This is an example of transgender discrimination. But things are slowly changing. For example, the United States Departments of Education and Justice require that schools respect gender identities by referring to students by their preferred names and pronouns, such as he, she, they, and X. It also requires that transgender students be allowed to use the bathrooms that fit their gender identity. In Canada, a proposed **bill** would add gender identity and gender expression as a protected ground in the Canadian Human Right's Act. This would mean that no person can be discriminated against because of their gender identity.

It is important for everyone to respect and accept people no matter what their gender identity is. Understanding your gender identity can take a very long time and sometimes people can become very frustrated by it. Often, transgender people are worried that their families and friends might not accept their gender identity. It is important to always treat people equally, no matter what their gender identity is, so that they can feel comfortable and welcome in their community.

There are plenty of websites where you can find information. Try www.kidshelpphone.ca or hrc.org.

If you are questioning or having trouble understanding your gender identity or sexual orientation, it can sometimes help to talk about it with someone you trust. It can also be helpful to read about the experiences of others. Check your library for books or the Internet for helpful websites. It is important to understand that your gender identity is normal and natural, no matter where it falls on the gender spectrum.

FIGHTING FOR EQUALITY

Charities and organizations around the world are working to change the way that people view gender identity. These groups want to gain rights and acceptance for all people who identify as LGBTQ. There are countless organizations in North America that bring together different groups of people to fight for equal human rights for all people. For example, the organization Immigration Equality helps LGBTQ immigrants and refugees seek safety from countries where they are at risk of violence because of their gender identity. The Family Equality Council fights for equal rights for families in the LGBTQ community. Egale Canada Human Rights Trust is a charity that promotes LGBTQ rights through community education and engagement. Each of these organizations, and many others, are creating positive changes.

Pride organizations around the world have also helped to bring LGBTQ rights and acceptance to the public eye. In Toronto in 2016, Canadian prime minister Justin Trudeau participated in the Pride parade, bringing a lot of public attention to the event.

THINK ABOUT IT!

It is important to be accepting of other people's identities and be sure that we make our communities spaces in which people feel comfortable to express themselves. Think about how you might make your community a more accepting place with these questions.

1 What has shaped your identity? Have you expressed these parts of your identity in your community? If so, how? If not, what do you think your community could do to make you feel comfortable doing so?

2 What is the most important thing you feel you have learned about gender identity? Can you think of a way that your community could show support to LGBTQ people?

3 In what ways could you show support to someone who is questioning their gender identity?

GLOSSARY

activism	Actions that try to create social change
assigned	Designated or determined
bill	A proposed law in Canada
biological	Relating to the body and how it works
bisexual	A sexual orientation in which a person is attracted to both men and women
civilizations	The societies, cultures, and ways of life of certain areas
conventionally	Based on socially accepted beliefs or behaviors
cultural identity	A person's feeling of belonging to a group with a distinct culture
customs	Traditional ways of doing things that are specific to a certain culture
decriminalize	In a legal system, to remove something from being designated as illegal
discrimination	Treating someone unfairly because of race, gender, religion, sex, ability, age, and more
diverse	Having variety or many different types
dominant	Something that is influential, important, or powerful
ethics	Principles or values about what is right or wrong; a system of morals
gay	A sexual orientation in which a person is attracted to someone of the same sex; usually used to describe a man who is attracted to another man
gender identity	A person's own concept or understanding of their gender
homosexuality	Sexual attraction between people of the same sex
Indigenous	People who have lived in, or are native to, a region for a long time
lesbian	A sexual orientation in which a woman is attracted to another woman
morals	A person's standards of right and wrong behavior
physical attributes	The features of your body, such as your height and the color of your hair
pronouns	Words that take the place of a noun, such as a name
protests	An organized event where people express disapproval of something
respect	To think about others' feelings and give something the attention it deserves
sexual orientation	A person's sexual attraction to others
social identity	A person's sense of identity based on the social groups they belong to
socially constructed	Ideas that are created, or constructed, by the common knowledge and beliefs of people in a society
spectrum	A scale with extremes at each end
suppressed	To forcibly stop or hide; to exclude from public knowledge
unique	Being the only one of its kind
Western	Relating to Europe and America

INDEX